EMMANUEL JOSEPH

Tech Titans and Property Pioneers,
Personal Journeys in Business Mastery

Copyright © 2025 by Emmanuel Joseph

All rights reserved. No part of this publication may be reproduced, stored or transmitted in any form or by any means, electronic, mechanical, photocopying, recording, scanning, or otherwise without written permission from the publisher. It is illegal to copy this book, post it to a website, or distribute it by any other means without permission.

First edition

This book was professionally typeset on Reedsy.
Find out more at reedsy.com

Contents

1	Chapter 1	1
2	Chapter 1: The Visionary Spark	3
3	Chapter 2: The First Big Break	4
4	Chapter 3: Navigating the Competitive Landscape	5
5	Chapter 4: Building a Brand	6
6	Chapter 5: Scaling Operations	7
7	Chapter 6: Innovation and Adaptation	8
8	Chapter 7: Customer-Centric Approach	9
9	Chapter 8: Financial Acumen	10
10	Chapter 9: Leading Teams	11
11	Chapter 10: Overcoming Adversity	12
12	Chapter 11: Giving Back	13
13	Chapter 12: Reflections and Future Horizons	14
14	Chapter 13: The Art of Negotiation	15
15	Chapter 14: Embracing Technology	16
16	Chapter 15: Strategic Partnerships	17
17	Chapter 16: Personal Growth and Development	18
18	Chapter 17: Ethical Business Practices	19
19	Chapter 18: Balancing Work and Life	20
20	Chapter 19: The Legacy of Leadership	21

1

Chapter 1

Introduction

In the ever-evolving landscape of business, the worlds of technology and real estate have produced some of the most influential and pioneering minds of our time. "Tech Titans and Property Pioneers: Personal Journeys in Business Mastery" offers a captivating exploration of the lives and careers of these exceptional individuals. Through their personal stories, we gain valuable insights into the mindset, strategies, and resilience required to achieve extraordinary success. This book is a celebration of their journeys, filled with lessons that can inspire and guide aspiring entrepreneurs and business leaders.

Our journey begins with the visionary spark that ignites the entrepreneurial spirit. Each of our protagonists started with a dream, a unique idea that had the potential to disrupt industries and create new opportunities. Their early experiences, marked by challenges and setbacks, shaped their determination and creativity. These tech titans and property pioneers saw possibilities where others saw obstacles, and their unwavering belief in their visions set them on a path to greatness. Their stories serve as a testament to the power of ambition and the courage to pursue one's dreams.

As we delve deeper into their journeys, we encounter the pivotal moments that defined their paths to success. The first big break, the strategic decisions, and the innovative solutions they devised were not just products of chance but of meticulous planning and relentless effort. Their ability to navigate the competitive landscape and stay ahead of the curve is a testament to their strategic thinking and adaptability. By examining their milestones and breakthroughs, we gain a deeper understanding of the factors that contribute to achieving business mastery.

One of the key themes explored in this book is the importance of building a strong and authentic brand. Our tech titans and property pioneers understood that a brand is more than just a name—it's the essence of a company's identity and the promise it makes to its customers. Through their experiences, we learn about the creative processes, the challenges of establishing a market presence, and the efforts to build a loyal customer base. Their stories highlight the significance of consistency, authenticity, and storytelling in creating a brand that resonates with audiences.

Finally, this book delves into the personal growth and development of our protagonists. Achieving business mastery is not just about professional success—it's also about continuous learning, personal growth, and giving back to the community. Our tech titans and property pioneers share their journeys of self-discovery, the importance of mentorship, and their commitment to making a positive impact on society. Their reflections provide valuable lessons for anyone looking to leave a lasting legacy in the world of business. As we embark on this journey through their lives, we are reminded that true success is a blend of vision, perseverance, innovation, and a deep sense of purpose.

2

Chapter 1: The Visionary Spark

Every successful venture begins with a vision—a flicker of an idea that has the potential to transform the world. For our tech titans and property pioneers, this spark was fueled by their passion and a keen sense of future possibilities. They faced initial challenges and skepticism, but their unwavering belief in their vision propelled them forward.

This chapter explores the origins of their journeys, delving into the early inspirations and pivotal moments of insight. Whether it was a garage startup or a sketch on a napkin, these personal stories highlight the power of vision and the courage to pursue it. These pioneers dared to dream big and took the first steps to turn their dreams into reality.

Through interviews and anecdotes, we learn about the driving forces behind their ambitious goals. They share their experiences of overcoming self-doubt and external obstacles, emphasizing the importance of resilience and determination. The Visionary Spark sets the stage for the remarkable journeys that follow.

3

Chapter 2: The First Big Break

The path to success is rarely linear, and for our protagonists, the journey was marked by a series of breakthroughs. This chapter examines the critical milestones that set the stage for their meteoric rise. For some, it was securing their first major client; for others, it was a fortuitous encounter with a mentor or investor.

These moments were not just about luck—they were the result of relentless effort, strategic thinking, and a readiness to seize opportunities. Through detailed narratives, we explore how these breakthroughs shaped their businesses, instilled confidence, and provided the momentum needed to scale new heights.

The First Big Break emphasizes the importance of timing and preparedness. Our protagonists reflect on the lessons learned during these formative experiences, offering insights into the factors that contributed to their initial successes. This chapter underscores the significance of perseverance and the impact of key opportunities.

4

Chapter 3: Navigating the Competitive Landscape

In the world of technology and real estate, competition is fierce. The ability to navigate this landscape effectively can make or break a business. This chapter delves into the strategies employed by our tech titans and property pioneers to stay ahead of the curve.

From innovative product development to mastering the art of negotiation, their stories offer valuable insights into the tactical maneuvers that gave them an edge. We also discuss the importance of market research, understanding consumer needs, and the role of adaptability in an ever-changing environment.

Through case studies and personal accounts, we explore the challenges and triumphs of competing in a dynamic market. Our protagonists share their experiences of facing formidable competitors and leveraging their unique strengths. Navigating the Competitive Landscape provides a roadmap for success in a crowded field.

5

Chapter 4: Building a Brand

A strong brand is more than just a logo or a catchy slogan—it's the essence of a company's identity and the promise it makes to its customers. This chapter explores the branding journeys of our protagonists, highlighting the creative processes, the challenges of establishing a market presence, and the efforts to build a loyal customer base.

Through their experiences, we learn about the significance of consistency, authenticity, and storytelling in creating a brand that resonates. We also examine the role of social media and digital marketing in amplifying their reach and connecting with a global audience.

Building a Brand delves into the intricacies of crafting a compelling brand narrative. Our tech titans and property pioneers discuss the importance of staying true to their values and engaging with their customers in meaningful ways. This chapter emphasizes the power of a well-defined brand in achieving lasting success.

6

Chapter 5: Scaling Operations

Success on a small scale is impressive, but true business mastery involves scaling operations to meet increasing demand. This chapter focuses on the operational challenges faced by our tech titans and property pioneers as they expanded their businesses.

From hiring the right talent to optimizing supply chains, their stories provide a blueprint for managing growth effectively. We discuss the importance of leadership, delegation, and maintaining quality standards amidst rapid expansion.

Through in-depth interviews, we explore the strategies used to scale operations without compromising on excellence. Our protagonists share their experiences of navigating the complexities of growth and the lessons learned along the way. Scaling Operations offers practical insights for entrepreneurs aiming to expand their ventures.

7

Chapter 6: Innovation and Adaptation

Innovation is the lifeblood of any successful business, and our protagonists are no strangers to it. This chapter delves into the innovative solutions and groundbreaking ideas that set them apart from the competition.

We explore the role of research and development, the importance of staying ahead of industry trends, and the willingness to embrace change. These stories illustrate how innovation is not just about technology—it's about thinking differently and being open to new possibilities.

Innovation and Adaptation highlights the creative processes that drive progress. Our tech titans and property pioneers discuss their approaches to fostering a culture of innovation and the impact of disruptive ideas on their industries. This chapter underscores the importance of continuous improvement and forward-thinking.

Chapter 7: Customer-Centric Approach

A business is only as strong as its relationship with its customers. This chapter highlights the customer-centric philosophies that have been pivotal to the success of our tech titans and property pioneers.

We explore the strategies they used to understand and meet customer needs, the importance of exceptional service, and the impact of customer feedback. Through their experiences, we learn how building trust and fostering loyalty can drive long-term success.

Customer-Centric Approach emphasizes the value of empathy and active listening in creating a positive customer experience. Our protagonists share their stories of going above and beyond to meet customer expectations and the benefits of cultivating strong relationships. This chapter offers practical advice for maintaining a customer-first mindset.

Chapter 8: Financial Acumen

Sound financial management is a cornerstone of business success. This chapter examines the financial strategies employed by our protagonists to ensure profitability and sustainability.

We discuss their approaches to fundraising, investment, budgeting, and cost control. Their stories provide valuable insights into the financial decisions that fueled their growth and stability.

Financial Acumen delves into the intricacies of managing finances in a competitive environment. Our tech titans and property pioneers reflect on the importance of financial literacy, risk management, and the ability to make informed decisions. This chapter offers practical guidance for mastering the financial aspects of business.

10

Chapter 9: Leading Teams

Leadership is an art, and our tech titans and property pioneers have mastered it in their unique ways. This chapter delves into their leadership styles, the challenges of building and motivating teams, and the importance of creating a positive workplace culture.

Through their stories, we learn about the qualities that make an effective leader, the role of communication, and the impact of fostering collaboration and innovation within teams. Leading Teams explores the human side of leadership and the significance of emotional intelligence.

Our protagonists share their experiences of guiding their teams through periods of change and growth. They discuss the importance of trust, transparency, and empowering team members to achieve their best. This chapter provides valuable insights for anyone aspiring to lead with integrity and vision.

Chapter 10: Overcoming Adversity

No business journey is without its setbacks, and our protagonists faced their fair share of adversity. This chapter chronicles the obstacles they encountered and the resilience they displayed in overcoming them.

From economic downturns to personal challenges, their stories offer powerful lessons in perseverance, adaptability, and the importance of a strong support system. Overcoming Adversity highlights the strategies used to navigate tough times and emerge stronger.

Our tech titans and property pioneers reflect on the role of mental health and well-being in maintaining the stamina needed to face challenges. They share their experiences of finding strength in the face of adversity and the importance of staying focused on the bigger picture. This chapter underscores the value of resilience in achieving long-term success.

12

Chapter 11: Giving Back

Success is not just about personal achievement—it's also about making a positive impact on the community and the world. This chapter explores the philanthropic efforts and social initiatives of our tech titans and property pioneers.

We learn about their motivations for giving back, the causes they support, and the ways in which they leverage their resources to make a difference. Giving Back emphasizes the importance of corporate social responsibility and the fulfillment that comes from contributing to a greater good.

Through their stories, we see how business leaders can create meaningful change and inspire others to do the same. Our protagonists discuss the challenges and rewards of their philanthropic efforts and the lasting legacies they aim to leave. This chapter offers inspiration for those looking to make a positive impact through their work.

13

Chapter 12: Reflections and Future Horizons

As we conclude the book, we reflect on the journeys of our tech titans and property pioneers. This chapter offers their insights on what it means to achieve business mastery, the lessons they've learned along the way, and their visions for the future.

We explore the evolving landscape of technology and real estate, the emerging trends, and the opportunities that lie ahead. Reflections and Future Horizons provides a glimpse into the future of these dynamic industries and the potential for continued innovation and growth.

Our protagonists share their thoughts on the importance of continuous learning, staying true to one's values, and embracing change. They offer advice for the next generation of entrepreneurs and reflect on the enduring impact of their work. This chapter serves as a testament to the power of perseverance, vision, and the pursuit of excellence.

Chapter 13: The Art of Negotiation

Negotiation is a critical skill in both the tech and property sectors. Our protagonists have honed their abilities to strike deals, secure investments, and forge partnerships that drive their businesses forward. This chapter explores the techniques and strategies they use to negotiate effectively.

Through real-life examples, we delve into the preparation, communication, and persuasion tactics that lead to successful outcomes. We discuss the importance of understanding the other party's needs, finding common ground, and maintaining professionalism. The Art of Negotiation provides valuable insights for anyone looking to master this essential business skill.

Our tech titans and property pioneers share their stories of high-stakes negotiations and the lessons learned from both successes and setbacks. They emphasize the importance of building relationships and trust in the negotiation process. This chapter offers practical advice for navigating complex negotiations with confidence.

15

Chapter 14: Embracing Technology

Technology is a driving force behind innovation and efficiency in business. This chapter examines how our protagonists have embraced technological advancements to enhance their operations, products, and services. From automation to data analytics, technology plays a pivotal role in their success.

We explore the ways in which they have integrated technology into their businesses, from streamlining processes to improving customer experiences. Our protagonists share their experiences of staying ahead of the tech curve and the impact of digital transformation on their industries. Embracing Technology highlights the importance of staying current with technological trends.

Through case studies and interviews, we learn about the challenges and opportunities that come with adopting new technologies. Our tech titans and property pioneers discuss the importance of agility and the willingness to experiment with emerging tools and platforms. This chapter underscores the significance of technology in driving growth and innovation.

16

Chapter 15: Strategic Partnerships

Strategic partnerships can be a game-changer for businesses looking to expand their reach and capabilities. This chapter explores the alliances formed by our tech titans and property pioneers and the benefits of collaborative ventures. From joint ventures to strategic alliances, partnerships have played a crucial role in their growth.

Through detailed narratives, we examine the process of identifying potential partners, establishing mutually beneficial relationships, and navigating the challenges of collaboration. Our protagonists share their stories of successful partnerships and the lessons learned from both positive and negative experiences. Strategic Partnerships emphasizes the value of collaboration in achieving business goals.

We discuss the importance of alignment in values, goals, and expectations when forming partnerships. Our tech titans and property pioneers reflect on the role of trust, communication, and compromise in building strong alliances. This chapter offers practical guidance for entrepreneurs looking to leverage partnerships for growth and success.

17

Chapter 16: Personal Growth and Development

Business mastery is not just about professional achievements—it's also about personal growth and development. This chapter delves into the journeys of self-discovery and continuous learning undertaken by our tech titans and property pioneers. They emphasize the importance of personal development in achieving business success.

Through their stories, we learn about the habits, routines, and practices that have contributed to their personal growth. Our protagonists discuss the importance of self-reflection, goal-setting, and lifelong learning. Personal Growth and Development highlights the connection between personal and professional development.

We explore the role of mentors, coaches, and support networks in fostering personal growth. Our tech titans and property pioneers share their experiences of overcoming personal challenges and the impact of personal growth on their leadership and decision-making. This chapter offers inspiration for those looking to enhance their personal and professional lives.

18

Chapter 17: Ethical Business Practices

Ethics play a crucial role in building a sustainable and reputable business. This chapter examines the ethical principles upheld by our tech titans and property pioneers and the impact of ethical decision-making on their success. They emphasize the importance of integrity, transparency, and social responsibility in business.

Through real-life examples, we explore the challenges and dilemmas they have faced and the strategies used to navigate ethical issues. Our protagonists discuss the importance of creating a culture of ethics and the role of leadership in setting ethical standards. Ethical Business Practices highlights the significance of doing business with integrity.

We learn about the positive impact of ethical practices on reputation, customer trust, and long-term success. Our tech titans and property pioneers reflect on the importance of aligning business practices with personal values and the benefits of ethical behavior. This chapter offers practical advice for entrepreneurs looking to build an ethical and sustainable business.

Chapter 18: Balancing Work and Life

A chieving a balance between work and personal life is a challenge for many entrepreneurs. This chapter explores the strategies used by our tech titans and property pioneers to maintain a healthy work-life balance. They emphasize the importance of self-care, family, and personal fulfillment.

Through their stories, we learn about the challenges of managing demanding careers and personal responsibilities. Our protagonists discuss the importance of setting boundaries, prioritizing, and finding time for relaxation and hobbies. Balancing Work and Life highlights the significance of well-being in achieving long-term success.

We explore the role of support systems, including family, friends, and professional networks, in helping entrepreneurs maintain balance. Our tech titans and property pioneers share their experiences of navigating the pressures of entrepreneurship and the impact of work-life balance on their overall happiness and productivity. This chapter offers practical tips for achieving harmony between work and personal life.

Chapter 19: The Legacy of Leadership

As we near the end of our journey, we reflect on the lasting impact of our tech titans and property pioneers. This chapter examines the legacies they have built through their businesses, leadership, and contributions to society. They emphasize the importance of leaving a positive and enduring legacy.

Through detailed narratives, we explore the values and principles that have guided their actions and decisions. Our protagonists share their thoughts on the impact they hope to make and the legacy they aim to leave behind. The Legacy of Leadership highlights the significance of purpose-driven leadership.

We discuss the importance of mentorship, giving back, and inspiring the next generation of entrepreneurs. Our tech titans and property pioneers reflect on the lessons learned throughout their journeys and the enduring impact of their work. This chapter serves as a testament to the power of visionary leadership and the lasting contributions of our protagonists.

In today's fast-paced business world, technology and real estate have given rise to some of the most remarkable and trailblazing individuals we know. "Tech Titans and Property Pioneers: Personal Journeys in Business Mastery" dives deep into the lives and careers of these incredible people. Through their unique stories, we'll uncover the mindset, strategies, and resilience it takes to reach phenomenal success. This book isn't just about their triumphs—it's a celebration of their journeys, full of lessons that can inspire anyone aiming to make their mark in the business world.

Our story starts with that initial spark of inspiration that every entrepreneur knows so well. Each of our tech titans and property pioneers began with a bold idea, driven by their passion and foresight. They encountered challenges and doubt, but their unwavering belief in their vision kept them moving forward. These early experiences, whether in a garage startup or sketched out on a napkin, highlight the power of dreams and the courage it takes to chase them.

As we follow their paths, we'll see how pivotal moments shaped their success. Whether it was landing a major client or finding the right mentor, these breakthroughs weren't just lucky—they came from hard work and smart thinking. Our protagonists navigated the competitive landscape with savvy and adaptability, teaching us valuable lessons about timing, preparedness, and the ability to seize opportunities as they come.

One major theme we'll explore is the art of building a strong and authentic brand. These leaders knew that a brand is much more than a logo or a slogan—it's the heart of a company's identity. Their journeys show us the creative processes and challenges of establishing a market presence and building a loyal customer base. Consistency, authenticity, and storytelling were key to creating brands that truly resonate.

Lastly, this book delves into the personal growth that goes hand-in-hand with professional success. Our tech titans and property pioneers didn't just build businesses; they embarked on journeys of self-discovery, emphasizing the importance of continuous learning, mentorship, and giving back to their communities. Their reflections offer invaluable lessons for anyone looking to leave a meaningful legacy. As we journey through their lives, we see that true success blends vision, perseverance, innovation, and a deep sense of purpose

www.ingramcontent.com/pod-product-compliance
Lightning Source LLC
LaVergne TN
LVHW010445070526
838199LV00066B/6210